Biographies

Junípero Serra

Explorer and Missionary

by Tyler Schumacher

Consultant:
Iris H. W. Engstrand
Professor of History
University of San Diego
San Diego, California

Capstone *press*

Mankato, Minnesota

Fact Finders is published by Capstone Press,
151 Good Counsel Drive, P.O. Box 669, Mankato, Minnesota 56002.
www.capstonepress.com

Library of Congress Cataloging-in-Publication Data
Schumacher, Tyler.
    Junípero Serra : explorer and missionary / by Tyler Schumacher.
    p. cm. — (Fact finders. Biographies. Great Hispanics)
    Includes bibliographical references and index.
    ISBN-13: 978-0-7368-5440-5 (hardcover)
    ISBN-10: 0-7368-5440-1 (hardcover)
    1. Serra, Junípero, 1713–1784—Juvenile literature. 2. Explorers—California—Biography—
Juvenile literature. 3. Explorers—Spain—Biography—Juvenile literature. 4. Franciscans—
California—Biography—Juvenile literature. 5. Indians of North America—Missions—California—
Juvenile literature. 6. Missions, Spanish—California—History—Juvenile literature. 7. California—
History—To 1846—Juvenile literature. I. Title. II. Series.
F864.S44S38 2006
979.4'02'029—dc22   2005022582

Summary: An introduction to the life of Junípero Serra, the Spanish explorer and
    missionary who established nine missions along the California coast.

Editorial Credits
Megan Schoeneberger, editor; Juliette Peters, set designer; Linda Clavel and Scott Thoms,
    book designers; Wanda Winch, photo researcher/photo editor

Photo Credits
Collection of the Hearst Art Gallery, Saint Mary's College of California, Gift of Mr. and Mrs. Albert
T. Shine Jr., 26; The Granger Collection, New York, 4–5, 23; Image courtesy of the University of San
Diego, 19; J. Taylor Gallery/Jodie Taylor, 22; Leon Trousset (attr.), *Father Serra Celebrates Mass at
Monterey*, ca. 1870. Oil on canvas. California Historical Society, Fine Arts Collection, FN-31586, 21;
Library of Congress, 16; Mary Evans Picture Library, 12; The New York Public Library, Astor, Lenox
and Tilden Foundations, 10–11; The New York Public Library, Astor, Lenox and Tilden Foundations,
Photography Collection, Miriam and Ira D. Wallach Division of Art, Prints and Photographs, 13;
North Wind Picture Archives, 1; North Wind Picture Archives/Nancy Carter, 27; Photo courtesy of
Iris Engstrand, 8; Photo reproduced by permission of Patrick Tregenza, 6–7, 15; Photo reproduced
by permission of Patrick Tregenza, "Serra's Viaticum" by Mariano Guerrero, Oil on canvas, 1785,
Mexico, 25; San Diego Historical Society, Photograph Collection, 18; Stock Montage Inc., cover

1 2 3 4 5 6 11 10 09 08 07 06

Table of Contents

Chapter 1 The Road to San Diego 4

Chapter 2 A Simple Childhood. 6

Chapter 3 From Student to Teacher 10

Chapter 4 From Teacher to Missionary 14

Chapter 5 A Ladder of Missions. 20

Chapter 6 A Tireless Missionary. 24

Fast Facts. 27

Time Line. 28

Glossary. 30

Internet Sites. 31

Read More. 31

Index 32

The Road to San Diego

Pain shot through Junípero Serra's left foot. He could barely walk. For weeks he'd traveled through Mexico. But Serra refused to give up. Work awaited him in California. He planned to arrive at San Diego Bay by July 1769. Not even a sore foot could stop him.

After many days, Serra spotted San Diego Bay. San Diego's Indians looked on curiously. Serra had come there as a **missionary**. His job was to spread the **Catholic** faith. Now his work could begin.

Serra (standing, in robe) arrived at San Diego Bay on foot.

Chapter 2

A Simple Childhood

Junípero Serra's story starts on the island of Majorca. Majorca is in the Mediterranean Sea, about 100 miles (160 kilometers) east of Spain. Serra was born there November 24, 1713. His parents named him Miguel José Serra. Years later, he would become known as Junípero.

Serra's hometown, Petra, was a small farming village. In that village, Serra's family lived a simple life. Serra lived with his parents and sister in a stone house. It had rough floors and plain furniture. Serra's parents, Antonio and Margarita, grew crops and raised animals near the village. Serra learned farm work at a young age.

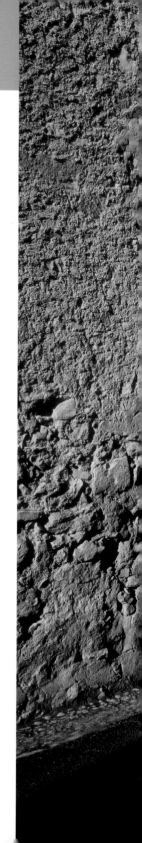

Serra grew up in this stone building in Petra, Majorca.

The Friars' School

Petra was a deeply **religious** place. Its people practiced the Catholic faith. The Convent of San Bernardino, a Franciscan school, was part of a church near Serra's home. Franciscans, also called **friars**, taught Serra reading, writing, math, and music.

St. Peter's Church in Petra, Majorca, was the church that Serra attended as a small boy.

Serra thought about joining the Franciscans. His parents were thrilled. But Serra was not yet a teenager. Friars only accepted boys older than 16. Serra had to wait.

The Smallest Friar

When Serra turned 15, his parents sent him to attend school in Majorca's capital city, Palma. The next year, Serra tried to join the Franciscans at the Convent of San Francisco in Palma. At first they said no. They feared he was too small to do the hard work at the school. Finally in 1730, the Franciscans allowed the small boy to try.

FACT!

Serra was very short. He couldn't reach the pages of the friars' large songbook. It rested on a music stand too tall for him.

Chapter 3

From Student to Teacher

Becoming a friar was not easy. New members had to spend their first year praying and doing chores. They cleaned the school and cared for the farm animals. They sang in the choir. They slept little. The friars discouraged letters and visits from family. New members were free to quit if they wanted. If they stayed, they became Franciscans.

Serra enjoyed the life of a friar. He read history books when he was not working or praying. Some books told of missionaries who traveled the world. He dreamed of becoming a missionary.

The Convent of San Francisco in Palma, Majorca, was where Serra studied to become a friar.

▲ Saint Francis, who founded the Franciscan order, was known for his love of animals.

A New Name

Serra became a friar September 15, 1731. He promised to work for God. As a sign of his promise, Serra changed his name. He chose Junípero, the name of a famous friar. Junípero had been a faithful friend of Saint Francis. Serra wanted to be just like the first Junípero.

Serra was now a Franciscan. But he still had to study to be a priest. For six years, he worked hard. In 1737, he passed his last exam. He got his degree from Lullian University in Palma.

Serra proved himself a good student and excellent priest. The Franciscans asked him to become a teacher. For many years, he taught other Franciscans to be priests. But he still dreamed of traveling to far-off places.

▲ Serra was a dedicated priest and teacher.

QUOTE

"Let us not be quiet. Let us speak our minds."
—Junípero Serra

Chapter 4

From Teacher to Missionary

Serra became a popular teacher and preacher. But he wanted to do more. He remembered the stories of famous missionaries. In 1749, he volunteered to work in Mexico's **missions**. He sailed for North America on August 28, 1749.

Serra first arrived in Mexico at the port city of Veracruz. He and Francisco Palóu, another friar, walked 200 miles (322 kilometers) to Mexico City. They carried no supplies. Kind people fed them along the way.

Serra (center) prayed with Francisco Palóu (right), his traveling partner from Majorca to Mexico.

The Pame Indians in Mexico fought against Spanish rule.

In Mexico, Serra lived among the Pame (PAH-may) Indians. He learned the Pame language quickly and translated prayers into Pame. He taught the Catholic faith through plays, songs, and ceremonies. Serra helped the Pame grow crops and build a church.

The Call to California

In the mid-1700s, Carlos III was the king of Spain. Spain claimed California, but few Spaniards lived there. The king feared Russia might take Spain's North American land. He ordered more missions in California. The missions would help Spain control the land and its American Indians.

In 1769, Serra was placed in charge of California's missions. San Diego and Monterey bays were selected as places to settle. Soldiers would go along with the friars and build forts to protect them.

FACT!

For most of his life, Serra slept only three or four hours every night. He spent most of his time praying, working, or traveling.

▲ Indians watched nearby as the friars built their mission at San Diego Bay.

Mission San Diego

Serra found San Diego a good place to live. It had a deep harbor and a river. Deer, antelope, and quail roamed the hills. Serra and the soldiers built small huts. They began trying to speak with the Indians.

But the San Diego mission did poorly. Fights broke out between the Indians and the missionaries. Food ran low. Governor Gaspar de Portolá was in charge of the soldiers. He told Serra that the group might have to leave San Diego.

On March 19, 1770, a ship from Mexico arrived. It brought food and tools. Mission San Diego survived.

The mission at San Diego survived food shortages and other problems. By 1846, stone buildings had replaced the original stick buildings. ⬇

Chapter 5

A Ladder of Missions

King Carlos' plan called for a second mission in Monterey. Later, he wanted several more to be built between there and San Diego. The missions would be like rungs on a ladder. They would spread Catholicism up and down California's coast.

Serra sailed north from San Diego to Monterey in April 1770. Because of storms, it took 40 days to sail 500 miles (805 kilometers). Once in Monterey, he started a mission named San Carlos.

Serra celebrated mass at a new mission in Monterey, California.

El Camino Real

Over the next 14 years, Serra helped start seven more California missions. Each one had its own friars and soldiers. A dusty path called the King's Road, or El Camino Real, connected them.

El Camino Real, or the King's Road, connected California's missions.

Serra traveled El Camino Real often. Along the way, he helped construct buildings, plant crops, and teach American Indians about the Bible. He gave orders to each mission's friars.

American Indians and the Missions

Life was difficult for Indians at the missions. Friars made them leave their villages and live at the missions. Mission Indians worked hard to grow crops and build churches. Some soldiers mistreated them. If the Indians broke a rule, friars whipped them. Hunger and diseases killed many Indians.

But Serra still believed becoming Catholic was good for the Indians. He continued his missionary work. He felt it gave Indians a place in heaven after death.

QUOTE

"The only good quality that I can feel sure I have, by the kindness and grace of God, is my good intention."
—Junípero Serra

Serra taught the California Indians about Christian symbols, such as the cross. ➡

Chapter 6

A Tireless Missionary

Serra kept traveling El Camino Real, even though his health began to fail as he grew older. By the 1780s, 18 friars and thousands of American Indians lived in California's missions. Serra continued to act as their leader. But by July 1784, old age forced him to stay at Mission San Carlos. He died in bed the next month.

Mission Accomplished

Serra traveled enough miles to circle the earth—more than Marco Polo or Lewis and Clark. He spread the Catholic faith to thousands. The missions he founded later became big cities like San Diego, Los Angeles, and San Francisco.

This painting shows Serra (right of priest, foreground) praying at Mission San Carlos shortly before his death.

▲ California artist
William Keith painted
many portraits of
famous Californians,
including this portrait
of Serra done in 1884.

Today, Serra has not been forgotten.
Streets, schools, and parks in California
bear his name. A statue of him stands
in the U.S. Capitol building. The
Serra International Club encourages
people to live a life of service. Serra's
memory lives on because of his tireless
missionary work.

FACT!

After Serra's death,
the Franciscans
founded 11 more
missions along El
Camino Real. All the
missions were spaced
one day's walk apart.

Fast Facts

Full Name: Miguel José "Junípero" Serra

Birth: November 24, 1713

Death: August 28, 1784

Hometown: Petra, Majorca

Parents: Antonio and Margarita Serra

Sibling: One sister, Juana

Religion: Roman Catholic

Education:
  Convent of San Bernardino, Petra
  Convent of San Francisco, Palma
  Doctoral Degree in Theology from Lullian
      University, Palma

Achievements:
  Established nine missions in California
  Spread Catholic faith to thousands

Time Line

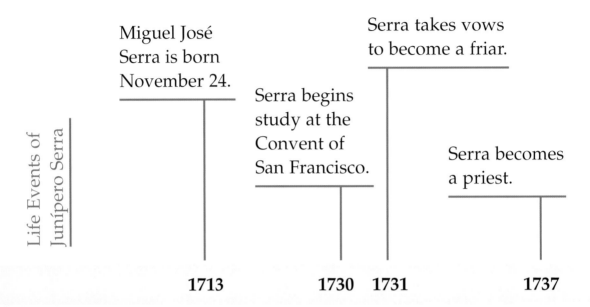

Life Events of Junípero Serra

Miguel José Serra is born November 24.

Serra begins study at the Convent of San Francisco.

Serra takes vows to become a friar.

Serra becomes a priest.

1713   **1730**   **1731**   **1737**

1607

Events in U.S. History

About 100 British colonists found Jamestown, the first permanent British settlement in North America.

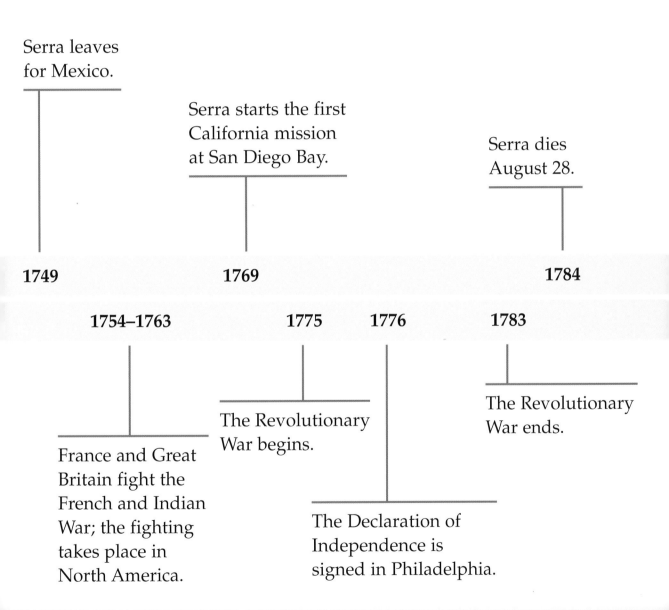

Serra leaves
for Mexico.

Serra starts the first
California mission
at San Diego Bay.

Serra dies
August 28.

1749

1769

1784

1754–1763

1775

1776

1783

France and Great
Britain fight the
French and Indian
War; the fighting
takes place in
North America.

The Revolutionary
War begins.

The Revolutionary
War ends.

The Declaration of
Independence is
signed in Philadelphia.

Glossary

Catholic (KATH-uh-lik)—having to do with the Roman Catholic church, a Christian church that has the pope as its leader

friar (FRYE-uhr)—a member of a religious group that owns no property and combines outside religious activity with a quiet, secluded life

mission (MISH-uhn)—a place built by a church for the purpose of spreading its faith

missionary (MISH-uh-ner-ee)—someone who is sent by a church or religious group to teach that group's faith and do good works, especially in a foreign country

religious (ri-LIJ-uhss)—having a system of belief, faith, and worship

Internet Sites

FactHound offers a safe, fun way to find Internet sites related to this book. All of the sites on FactHound have been researched by our staff.

Here's how:

1. Visit *www.facthound.com*
2. Type in this special code **0736854401** for age-appropriate sites. Or enter a search word related to this book for a more general search.
3. Click on the **Fetch It** button.

FactHound will fetch the best sites for you!

Read More

Bowler, Sarah. *Father Junípero Serra and the California Missions.* Proud Heritage. Chanhassen, Minn.: Child's World, 2003.

Heinrichs, Ann. *The California Missions.* We the People. Minneapolis: Compass Point Books, 2002.

Whiting, Jim. *Junipero Jose Serra.* Latinos in American History. Hockessin, Del.: Mitchell Lane, 2004.

Index

American Indians, 4, 16, 17, 18–19, 22–23, 24

California, 4, 17, 20, 21, 22, 23, 24
Carlos III, King of Spain, 17, 20
Catholicism, 4, 8, 16, 20, 23, 24
Convent of San Bernardino, 8
Convent of San Francisco, 9, 11

El Camino Real, 21–22, 24, 26

Franciscans. *See* friars
friars, 8–9, 10, 11, 12, 13, 17, 18, 21, 22, 24, 26

King's Road. *See* El Camino Real

Los Angeles, California, 24

Mexico, 4, 14, 15, 16, 19
Mexico City, Mexico, 14
missionaries, 10, 14, 19
missions, 14, 17, 20, 21, 22, 24, 26
    San Carlos, 20, 24, 25
    San Diego, 18–19, 20
Monterey, California, 17, 20, 21

Palma, Majorca, 9, 11
Palóu, Francisco, 14, 15
Pame Indians, 16
Petra, Majorca, 6, 7, 8
Portolá, Governor Gaspar de, 19

Saint Francis, 12
San Diego, California, 24
San Diego Bay, 4, 5, 17, 18
San Francisco, California, 24
Serra, Antonio (father), 6, 9
Serra, Juana (sister), 6
Serra, Junípero (Miguel José)
    birth of, 6
    childhood of, 6, 7, 8
    death of, 24
    education of, 8, 10, 11, 12–13
    as friar, 10, 12
    as missionary, 4, 14, 16, 18–19, 20–23, 24, 26
    name, 6, 12
    as priest, 13, 14
Serra, Margarita (mother), 6, 9
Serra International Club, 26

Veracruz, Mexico, 14